sea COLORING BOOK

This Book Belong To.......

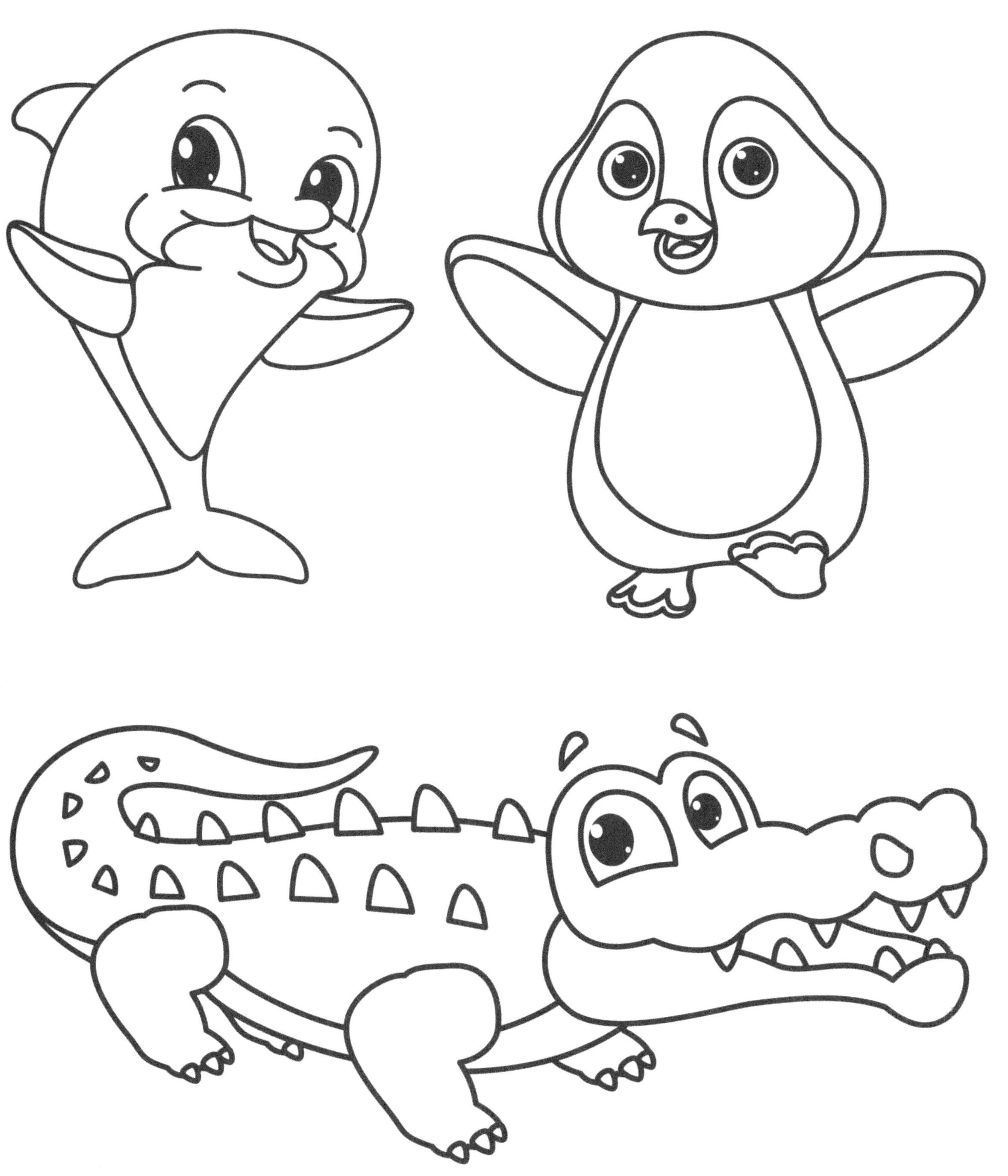

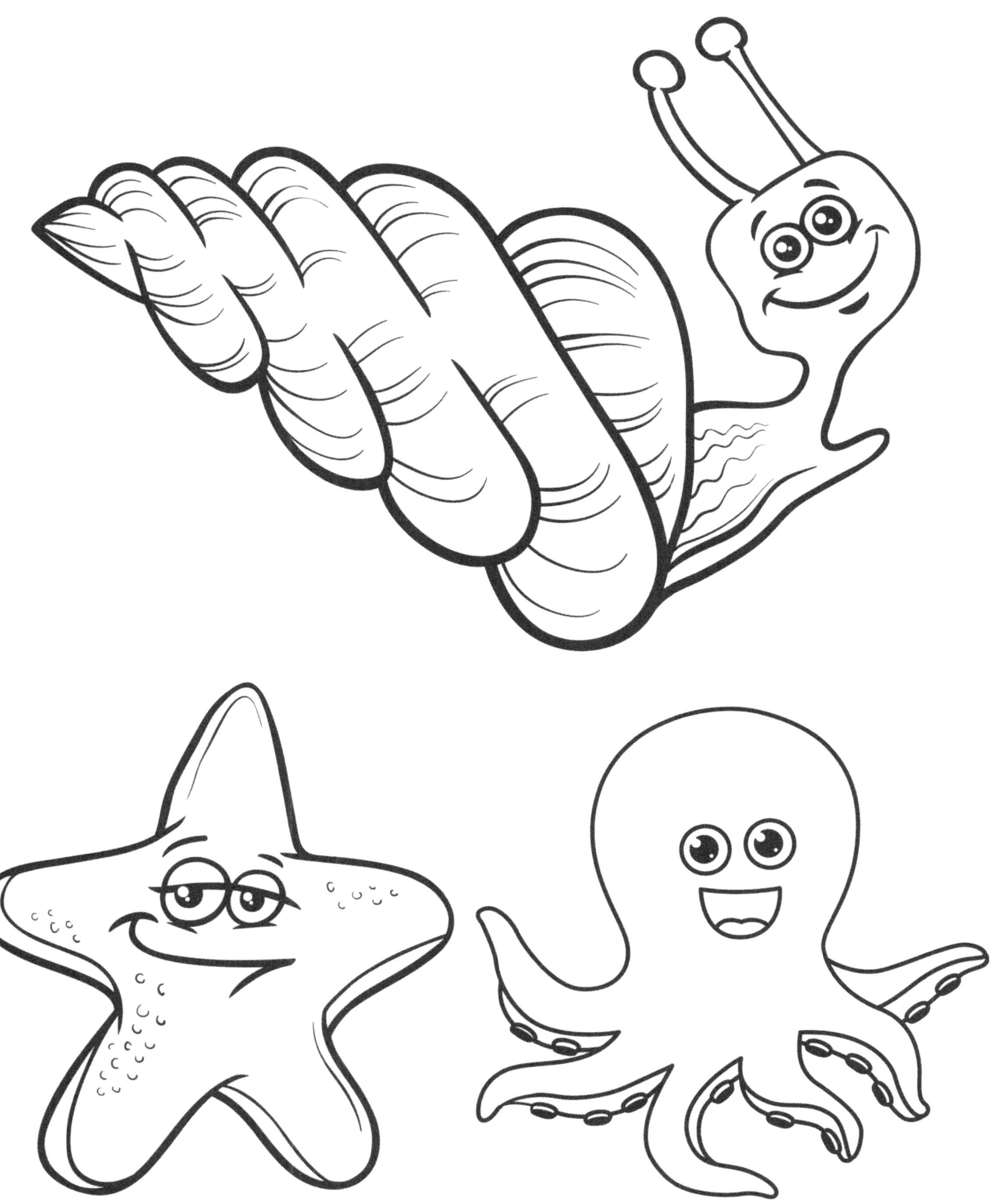

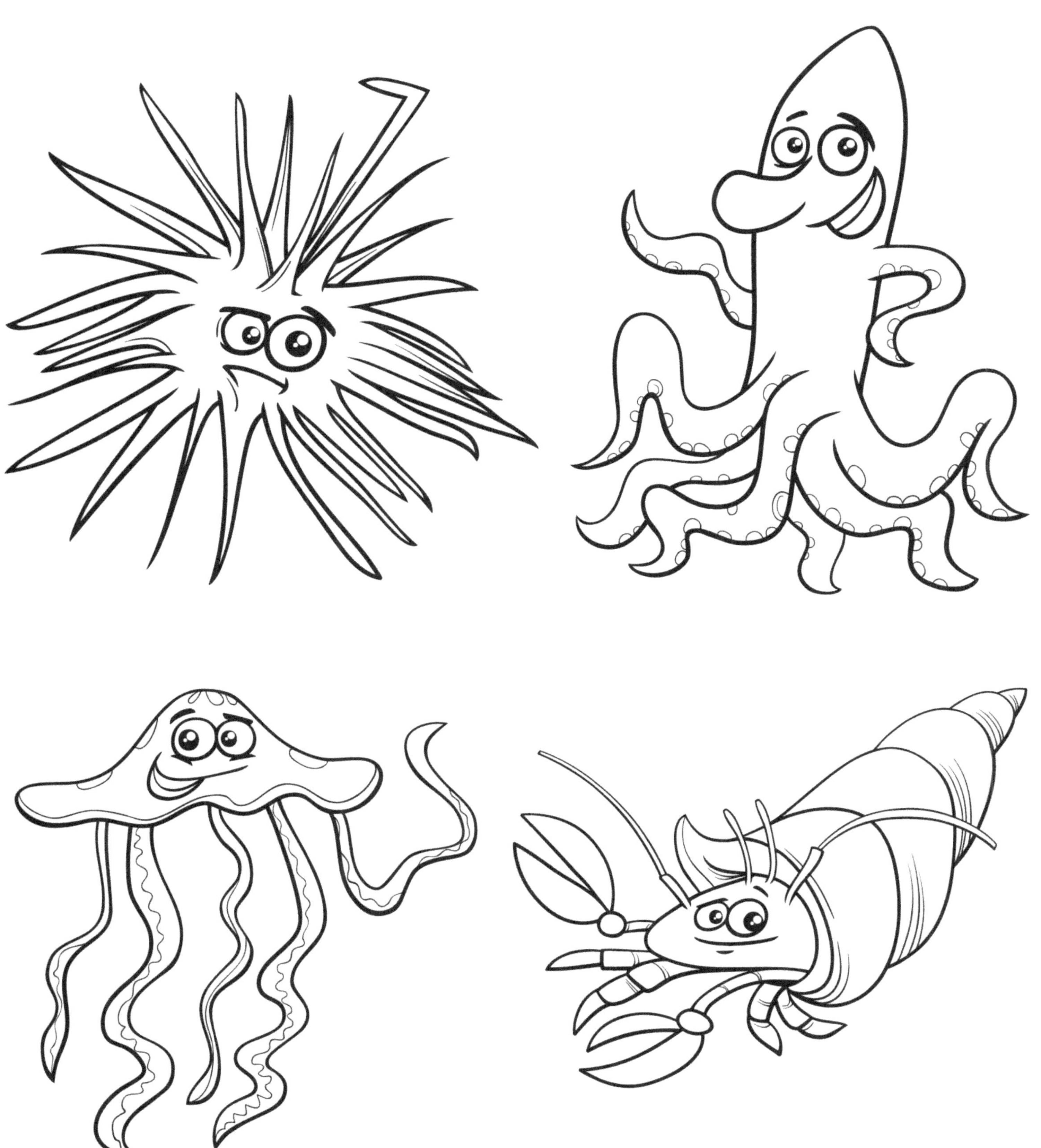

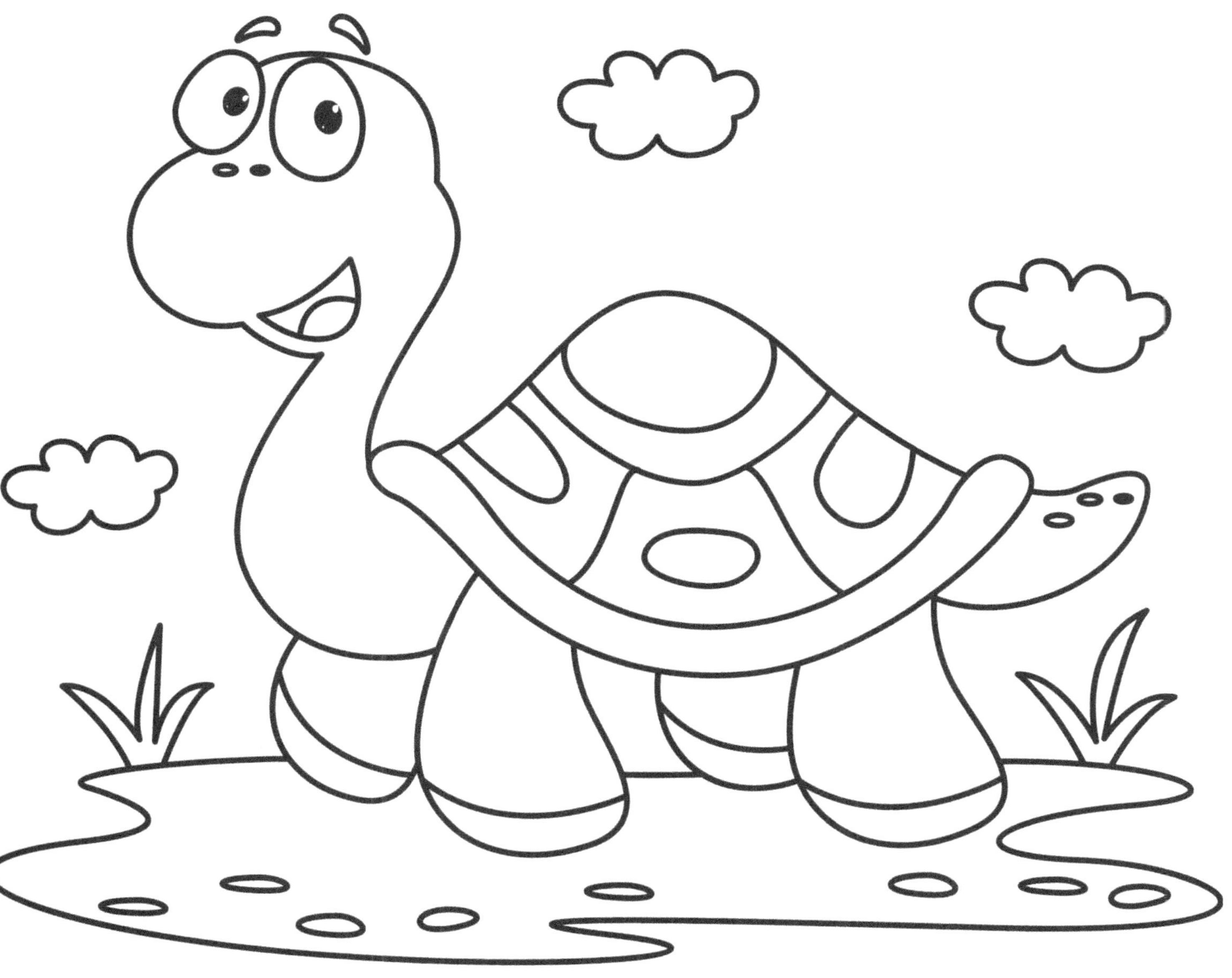

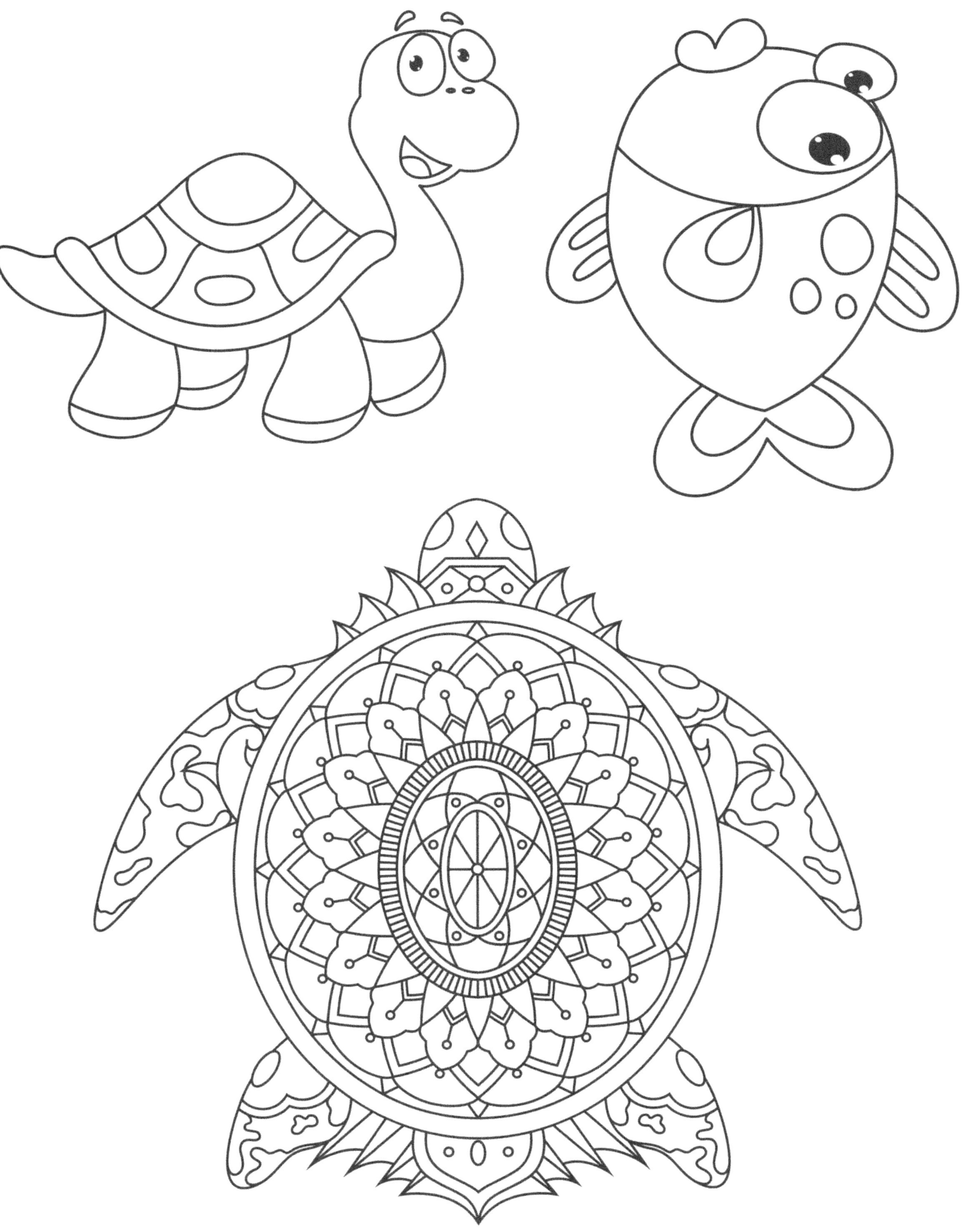

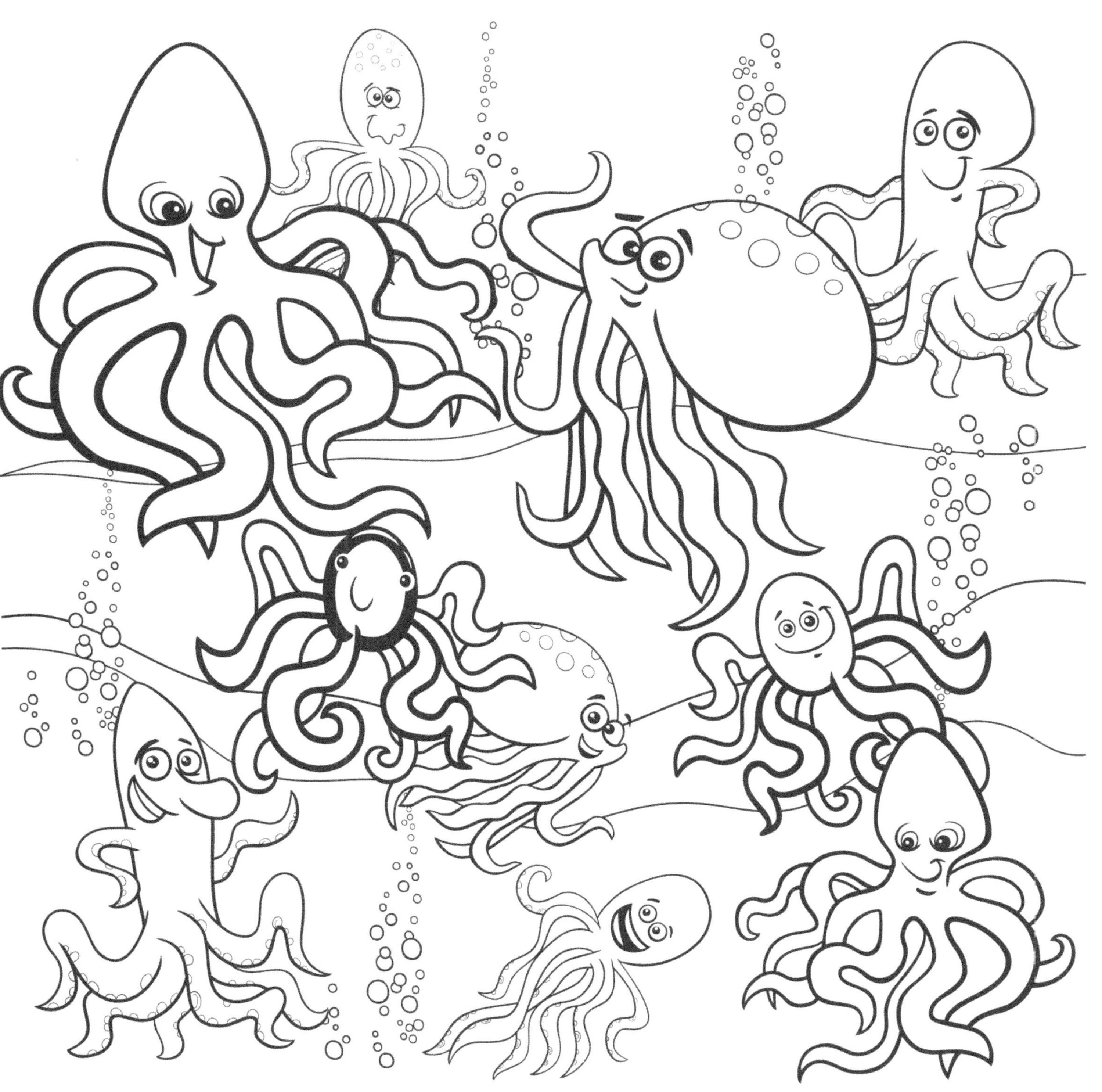

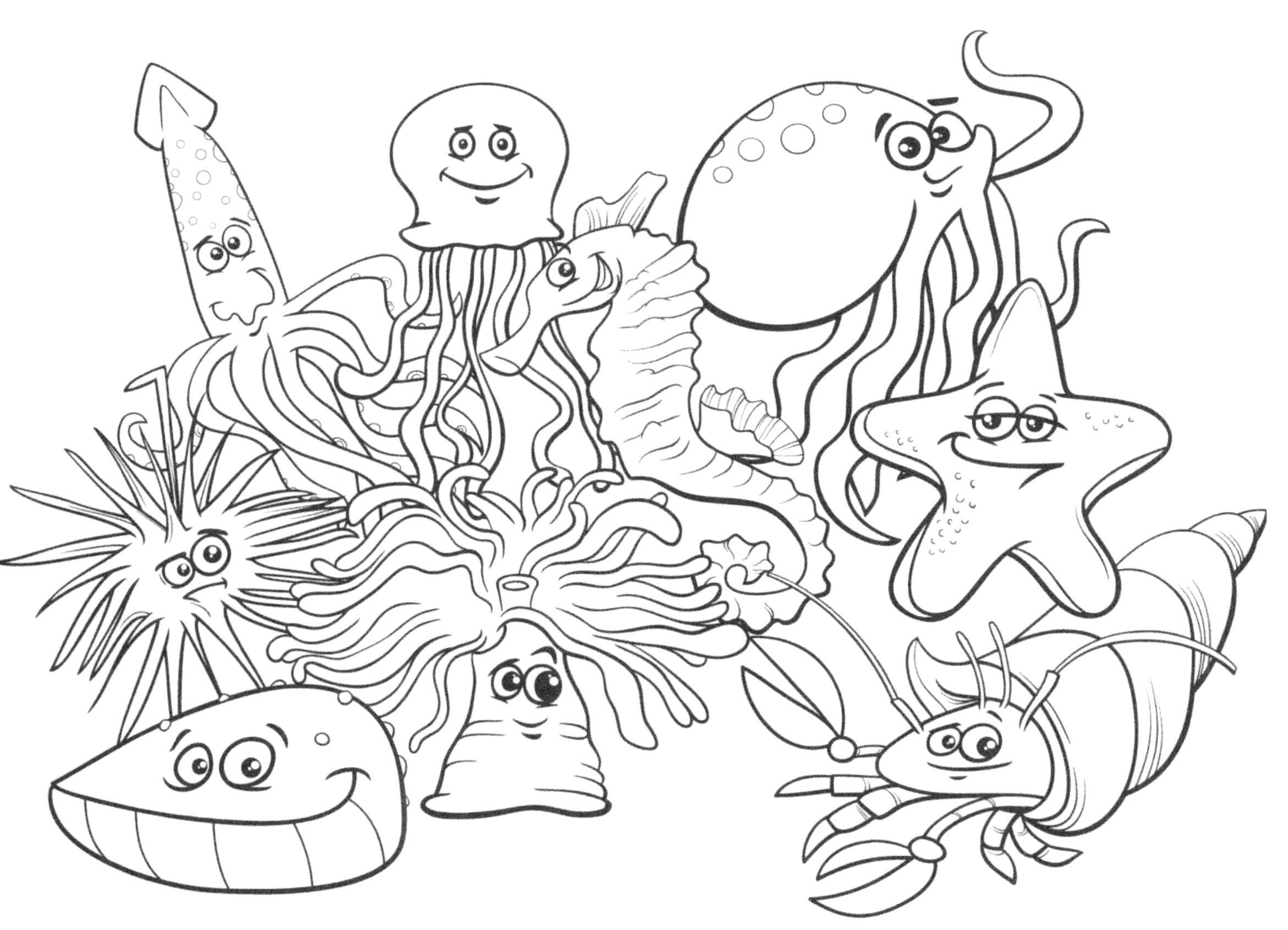

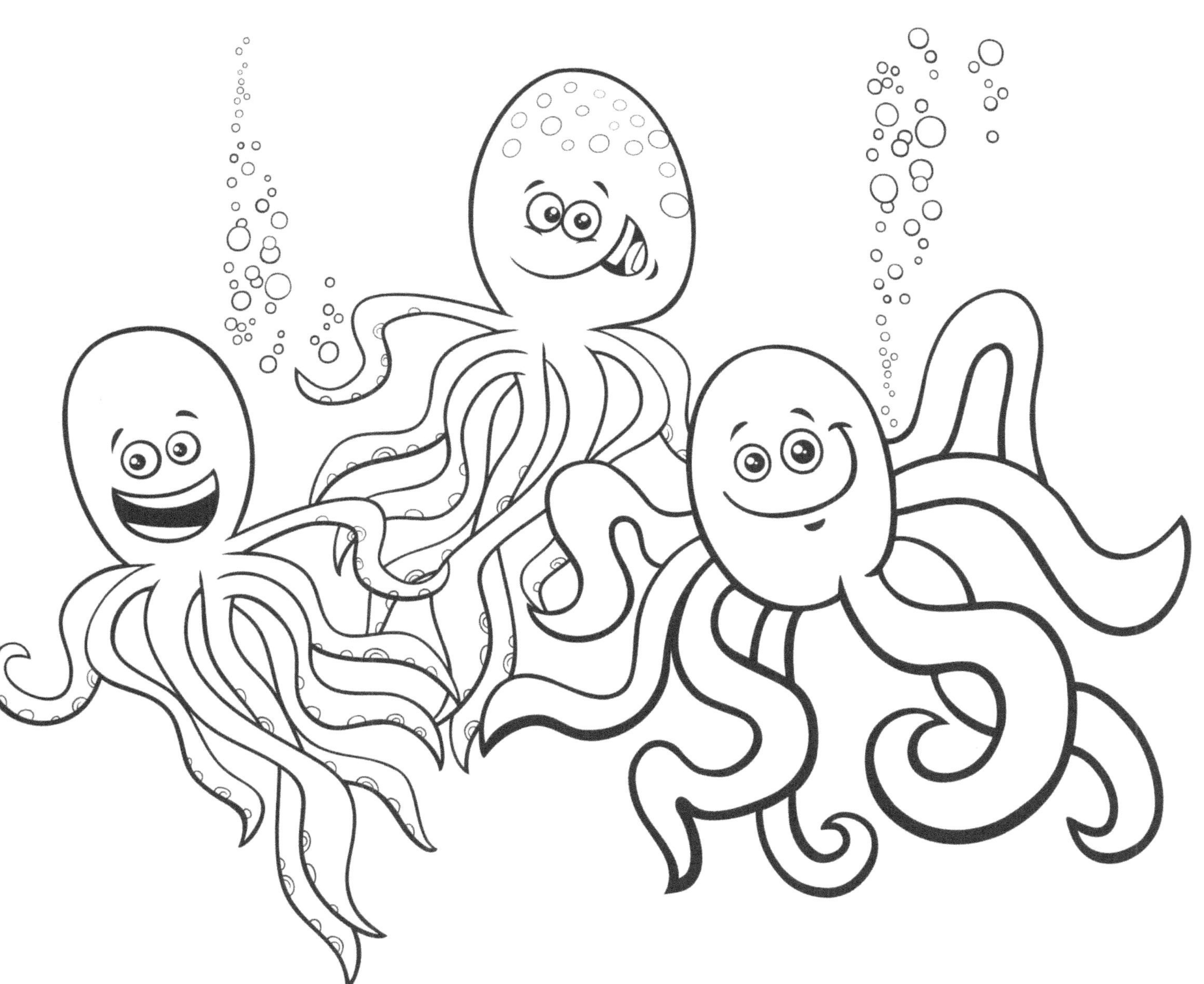

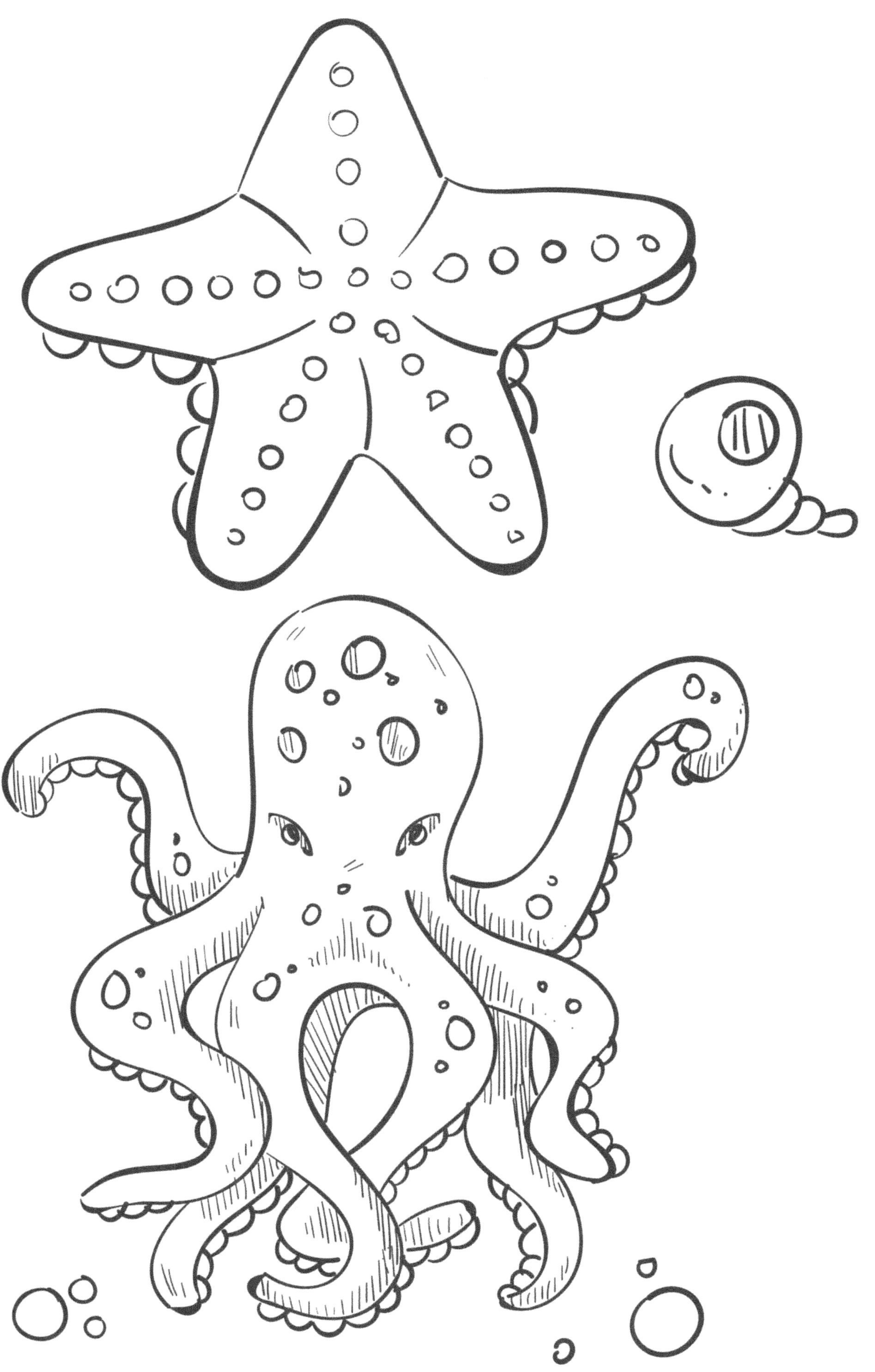

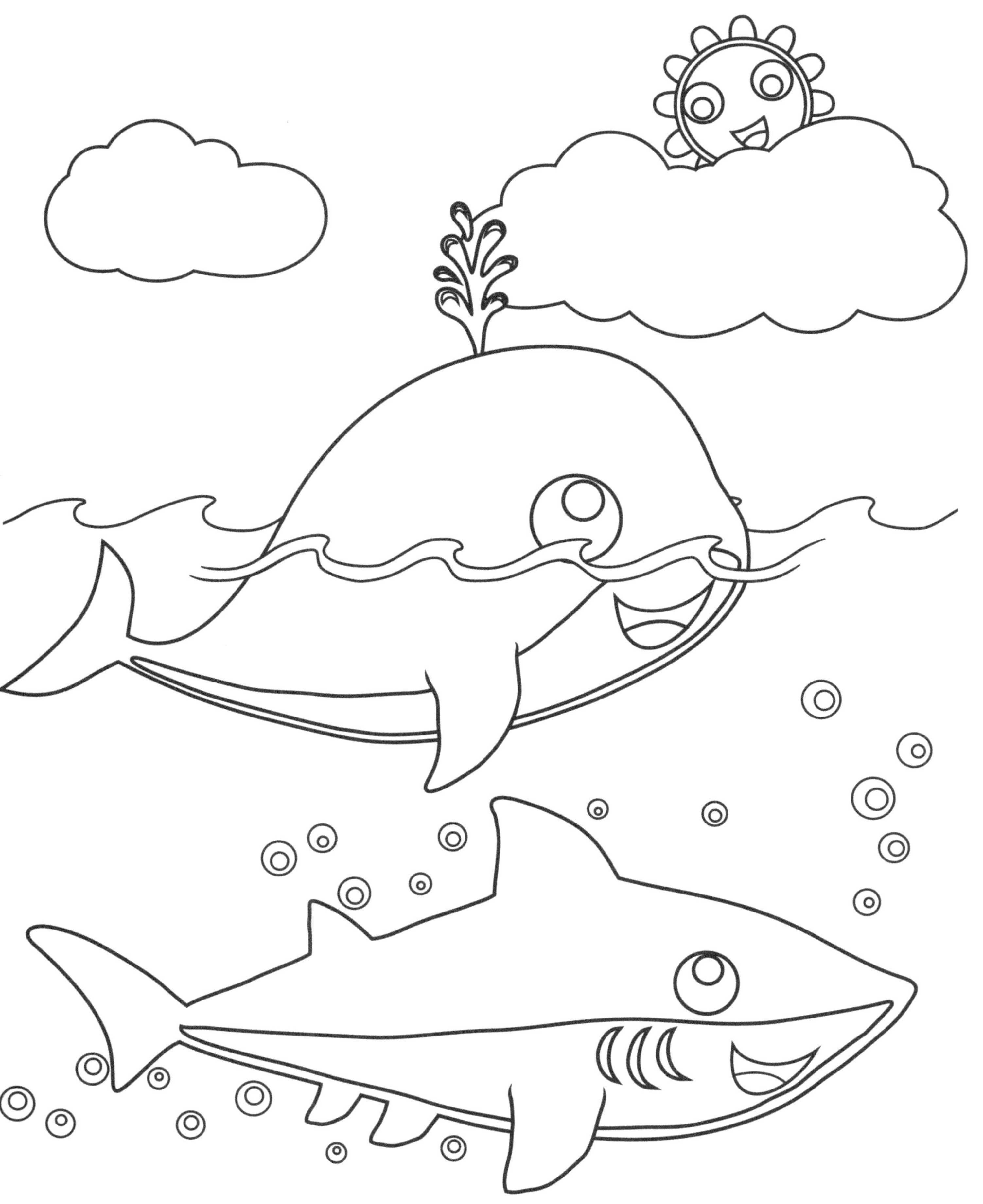

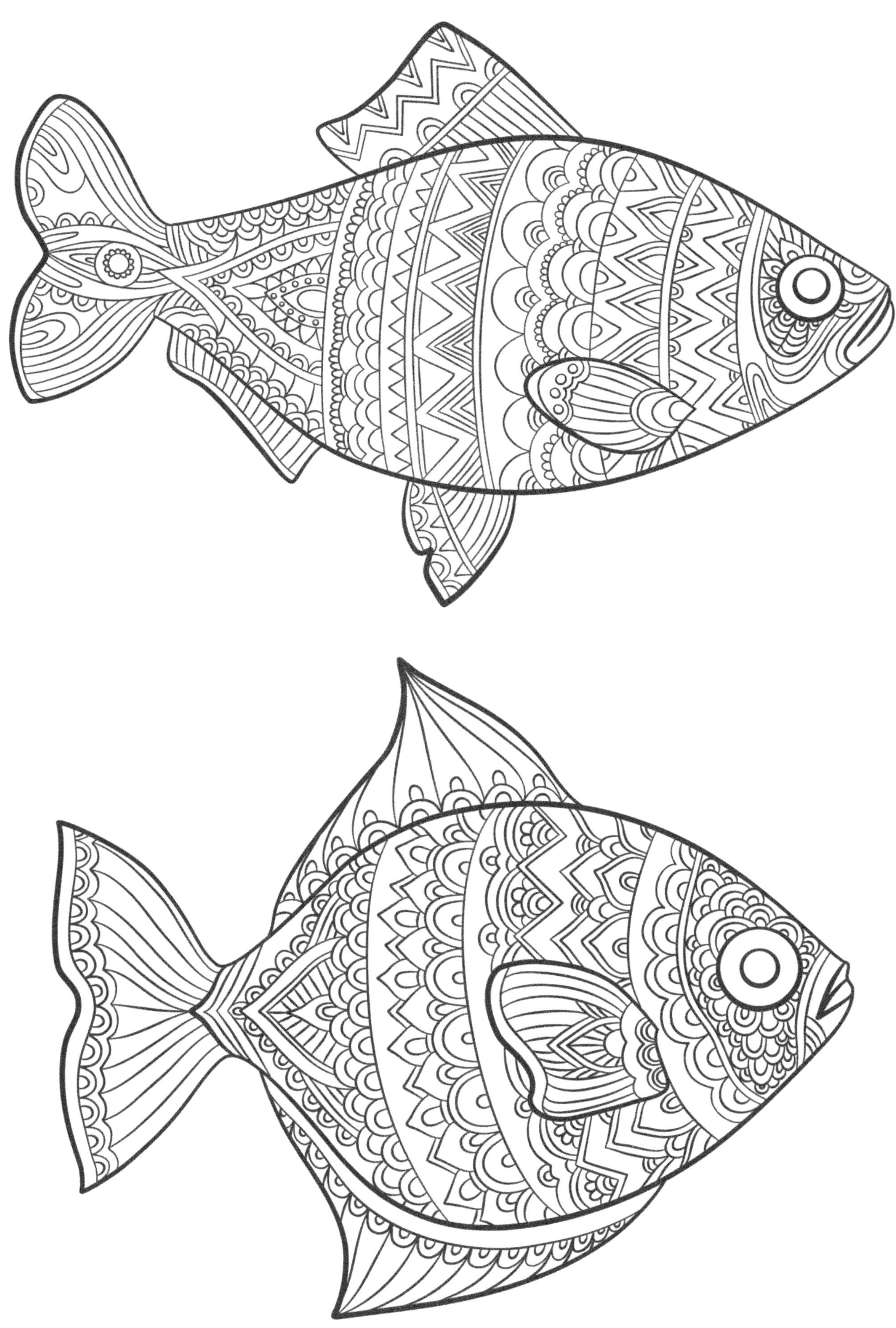

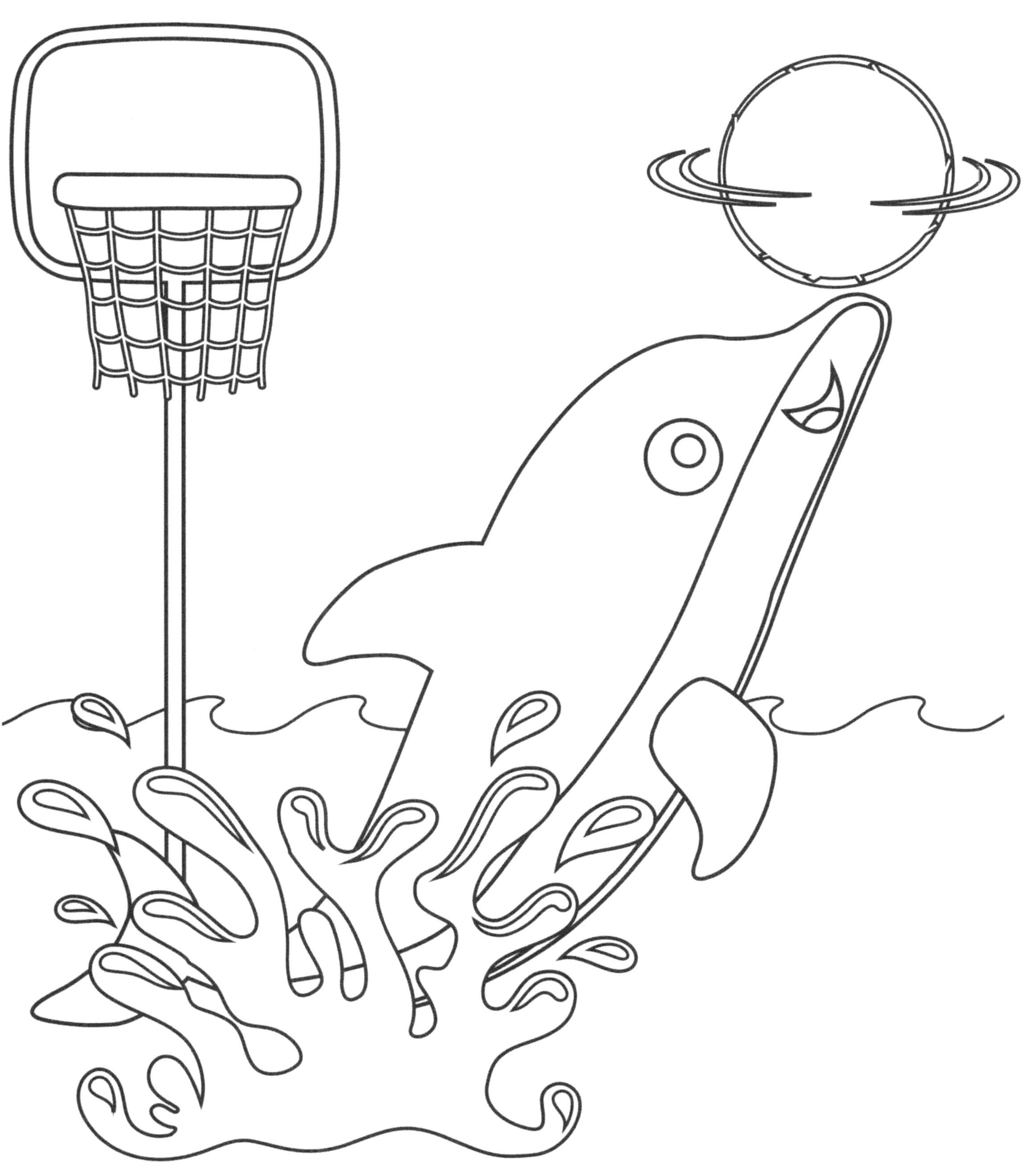

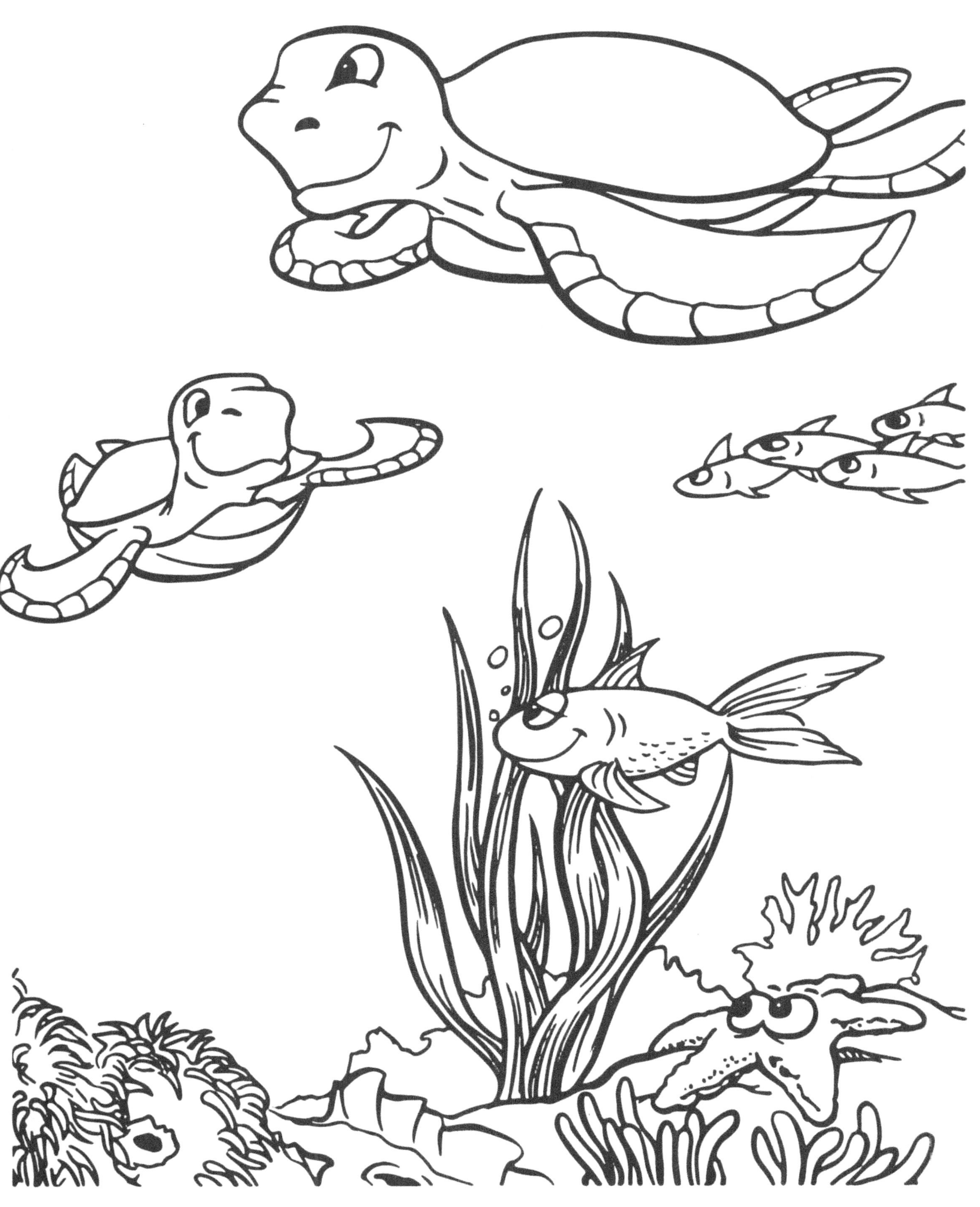

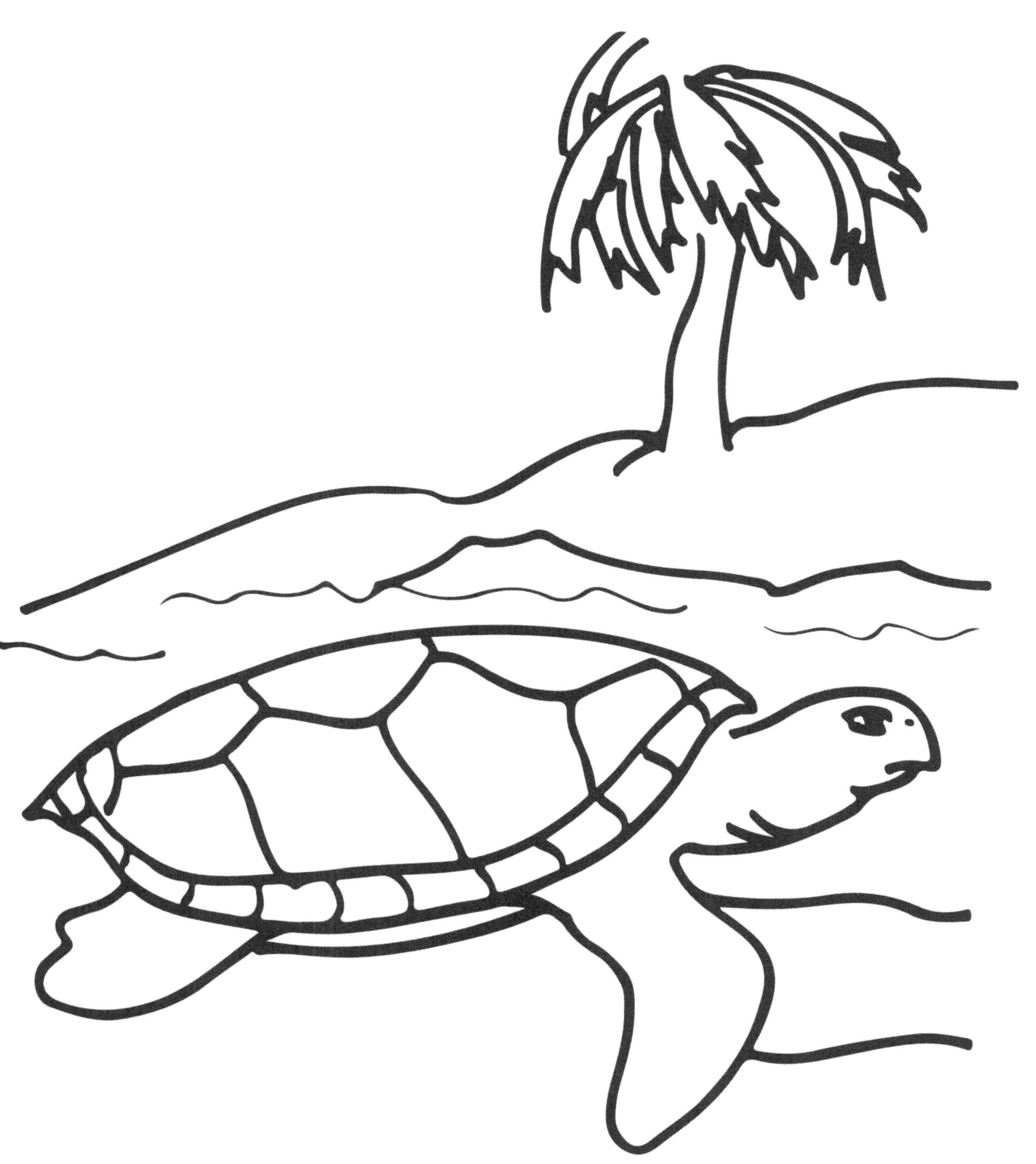

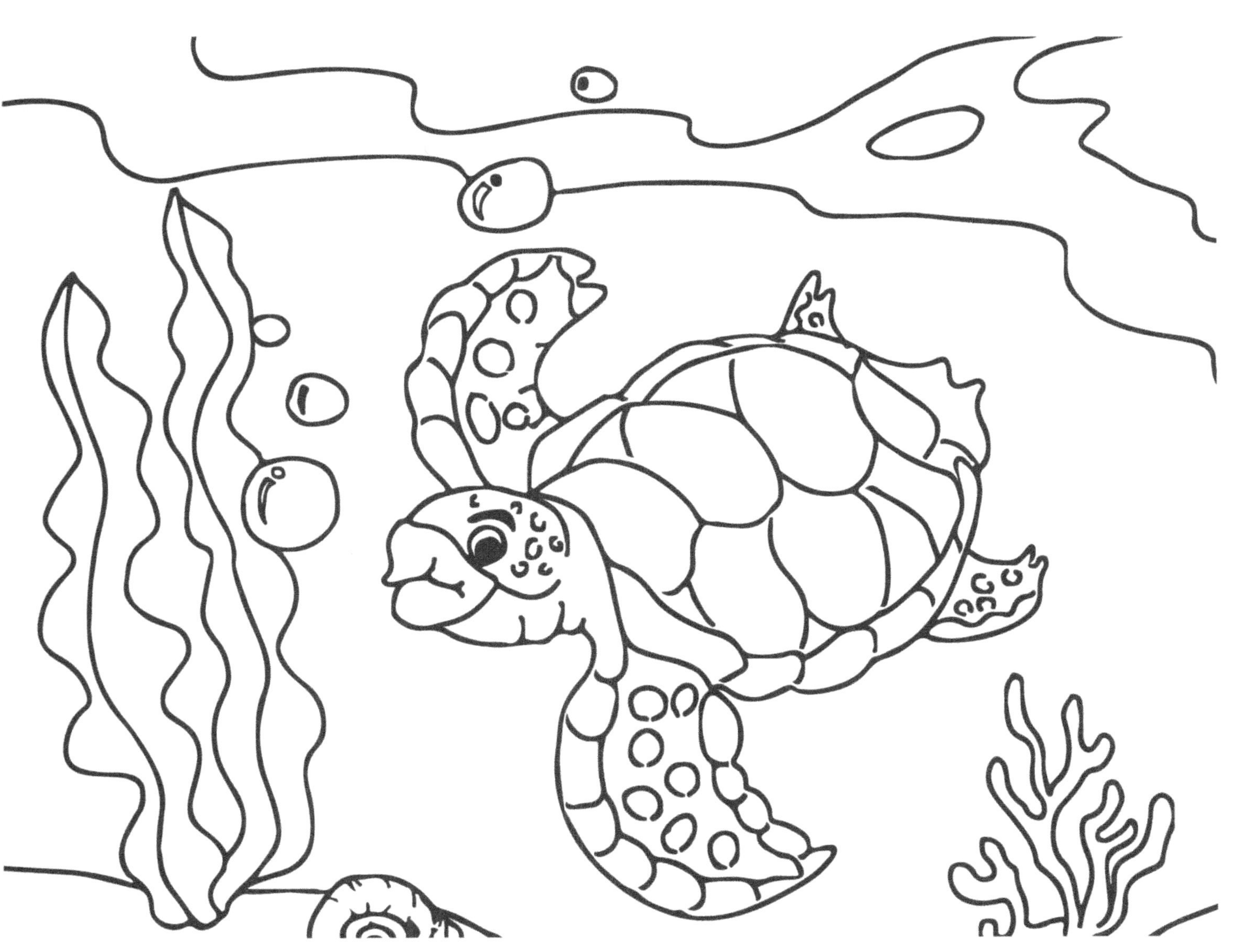

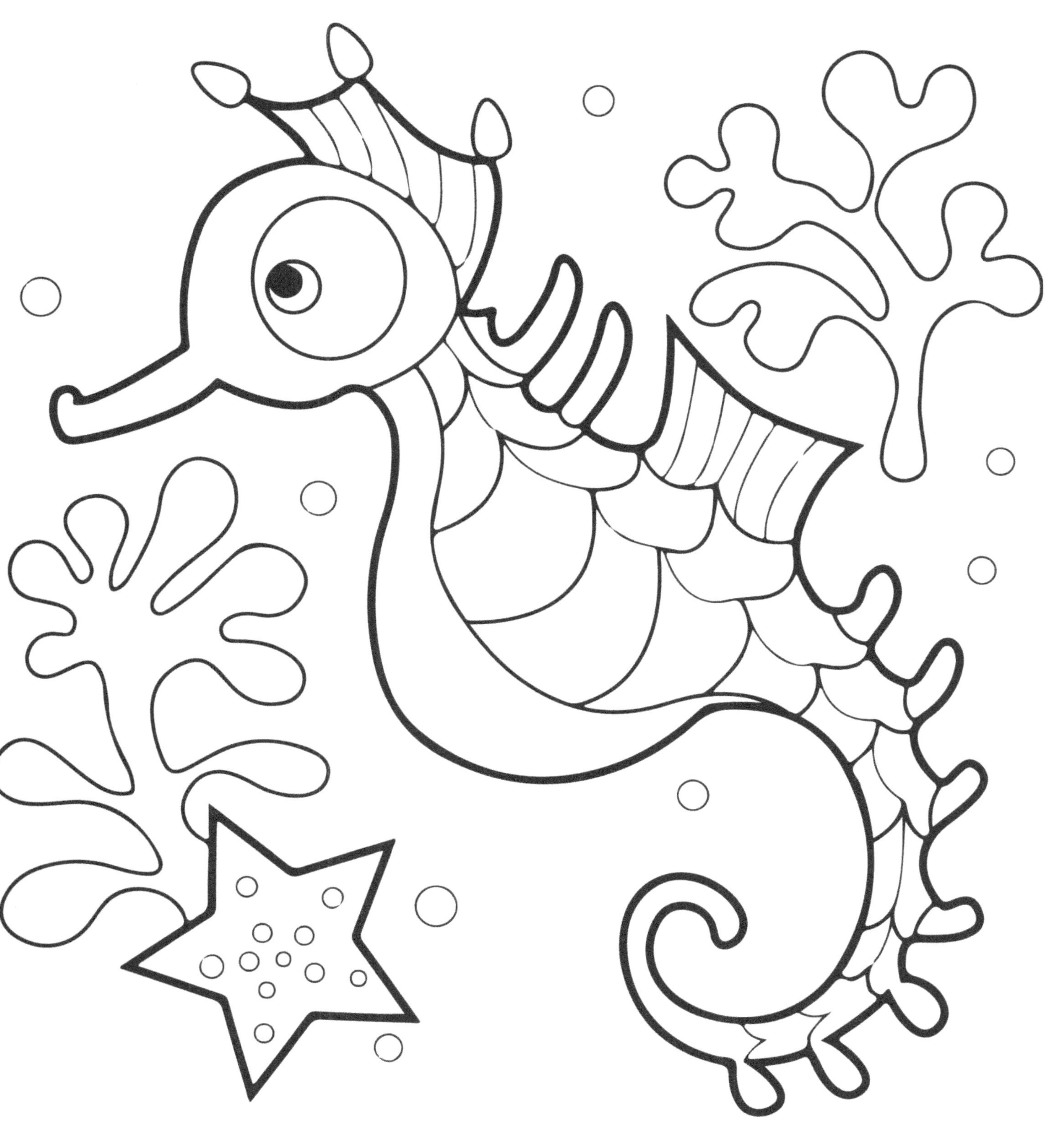

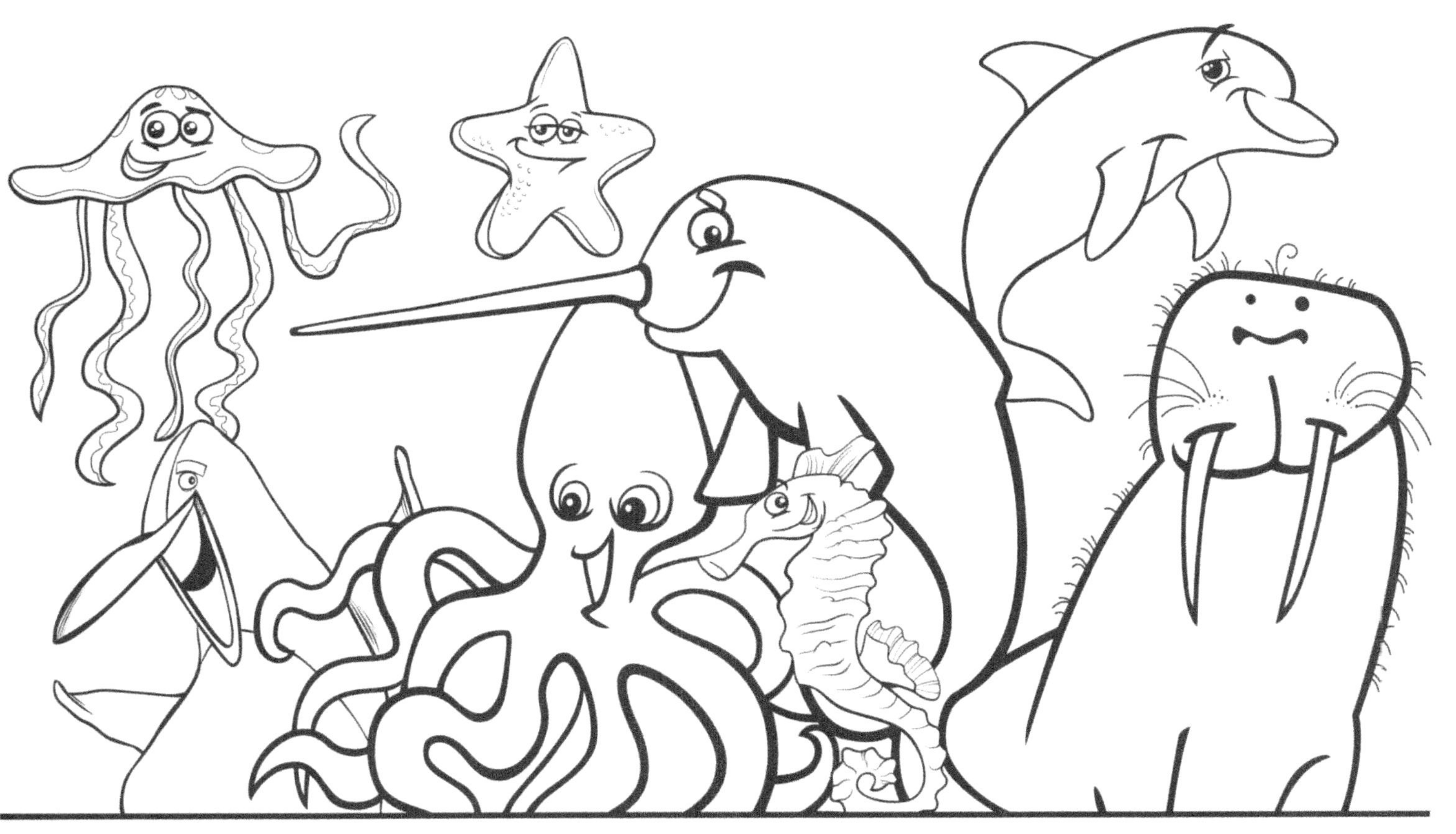

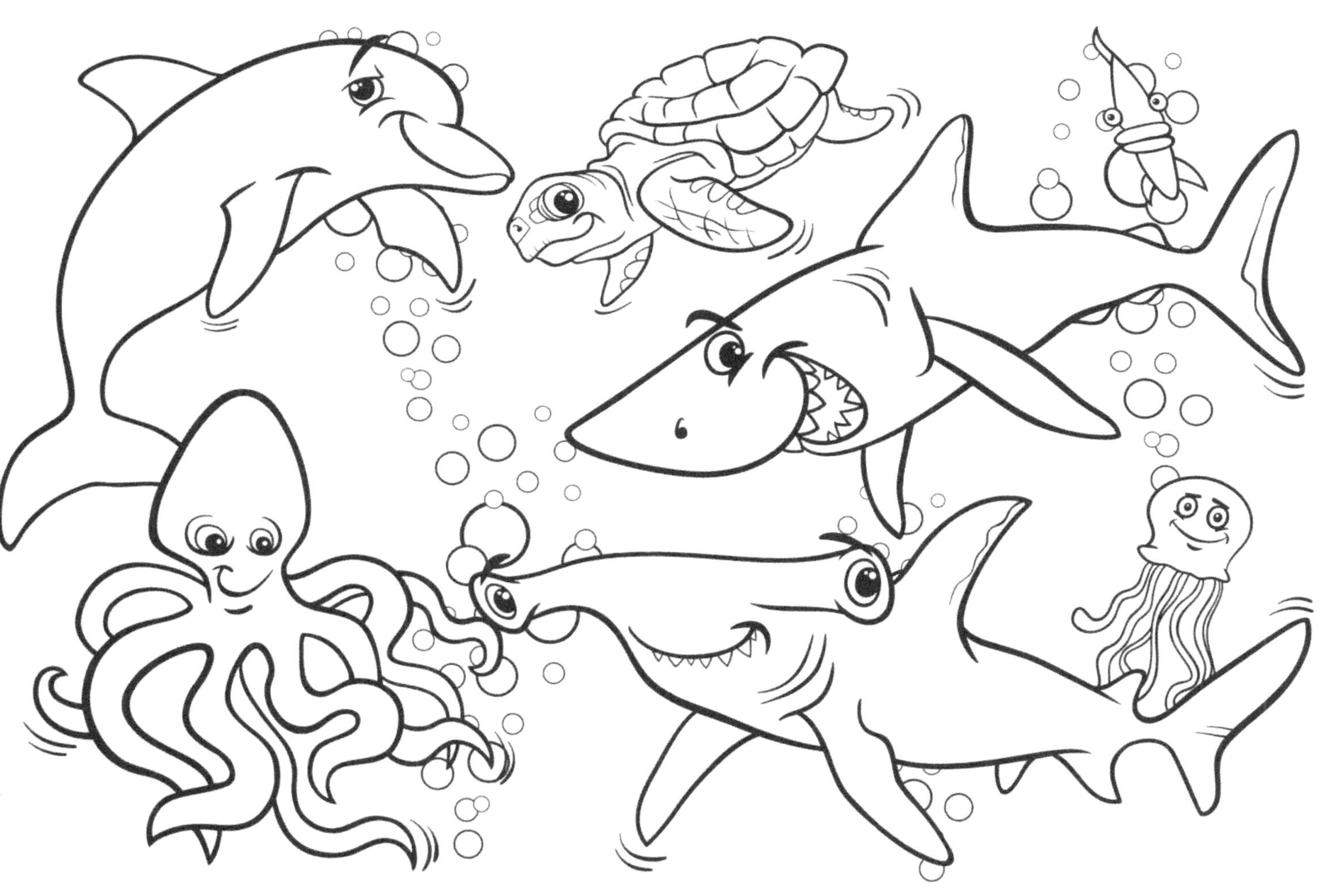

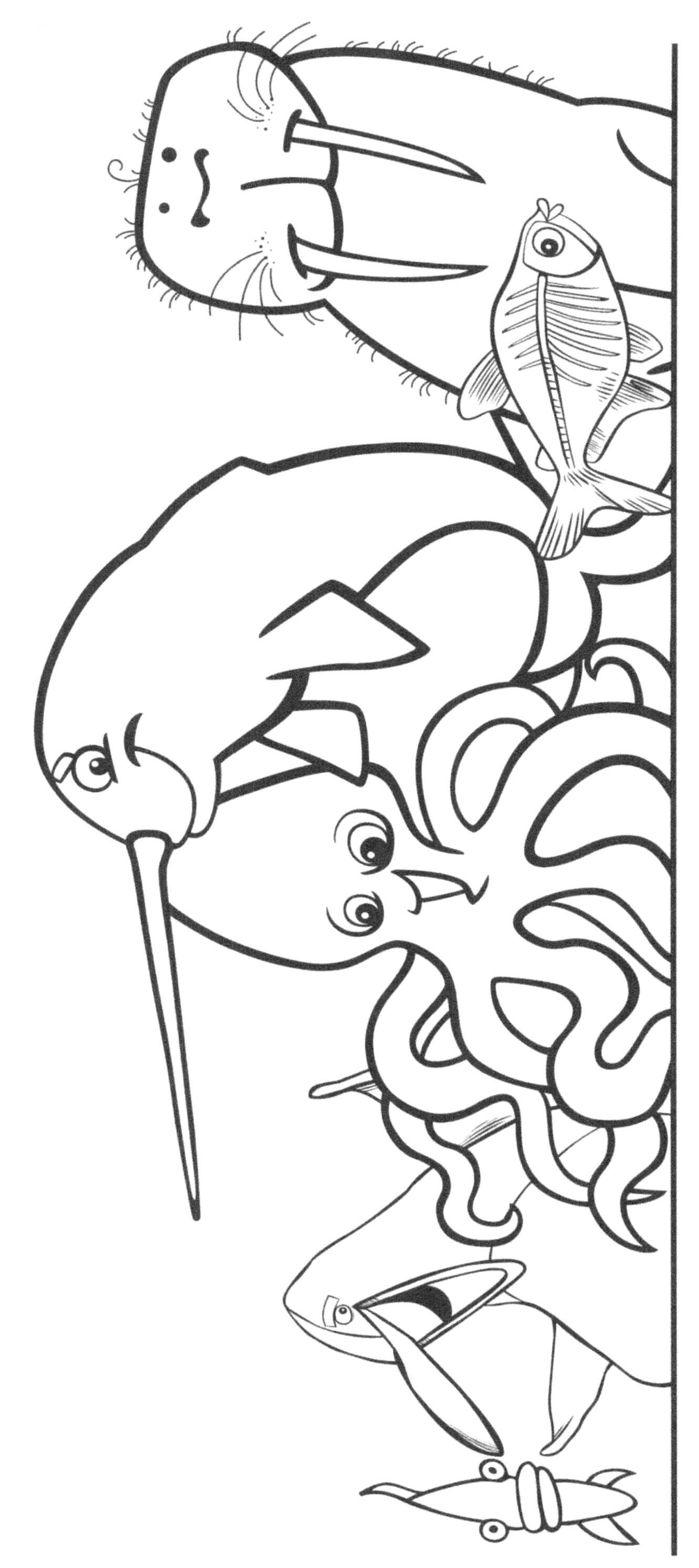

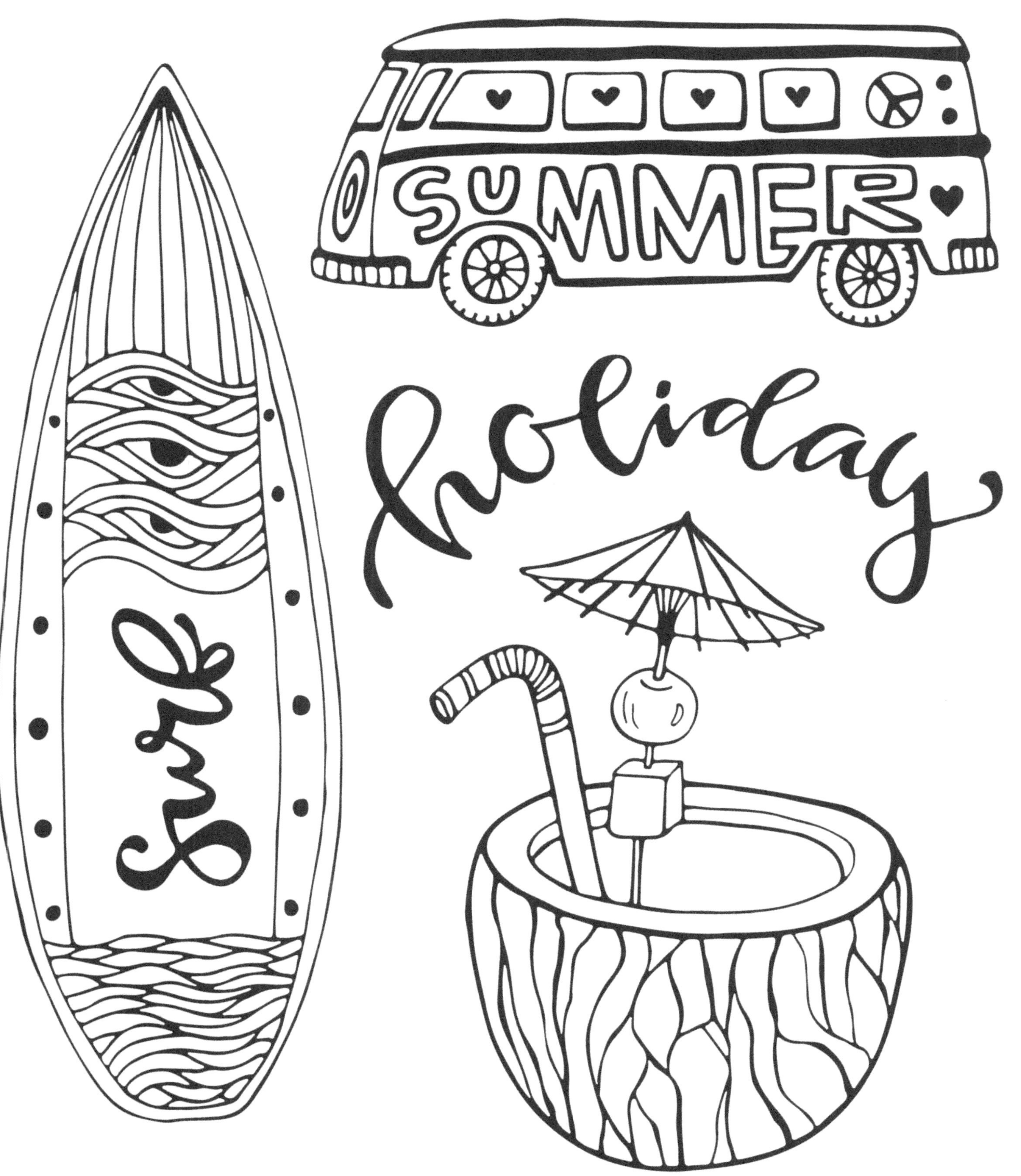

SUMMER
holiday
surf

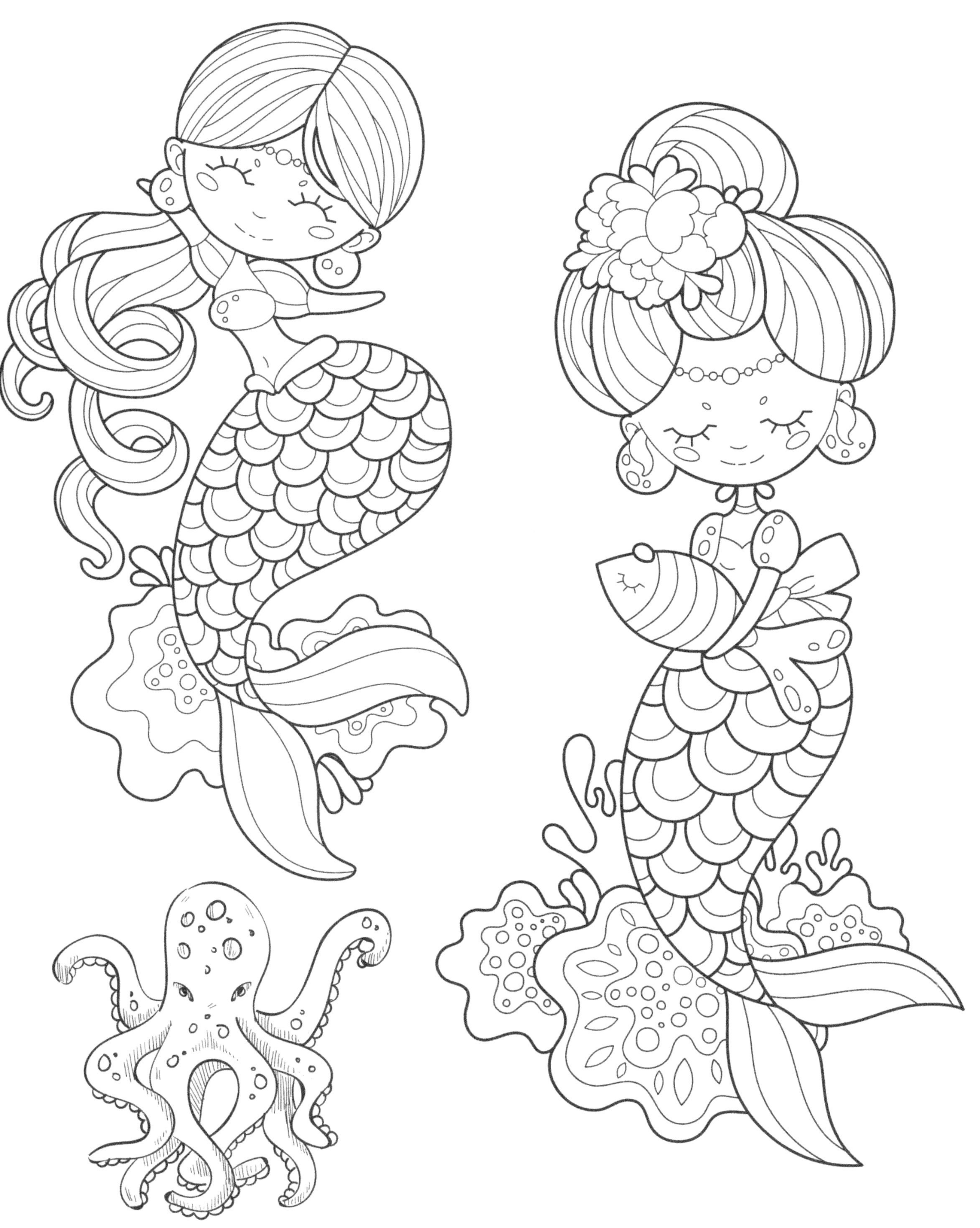

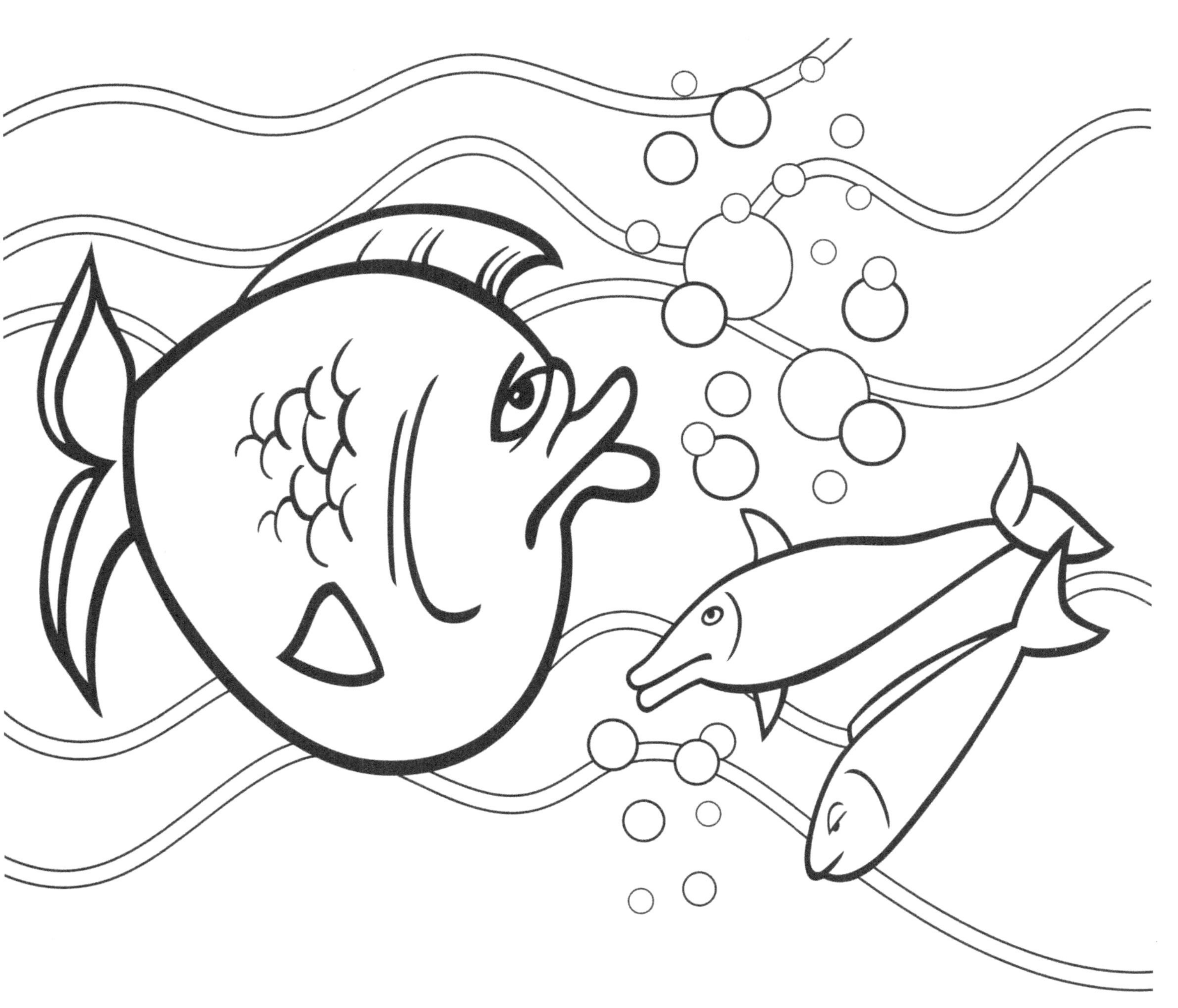

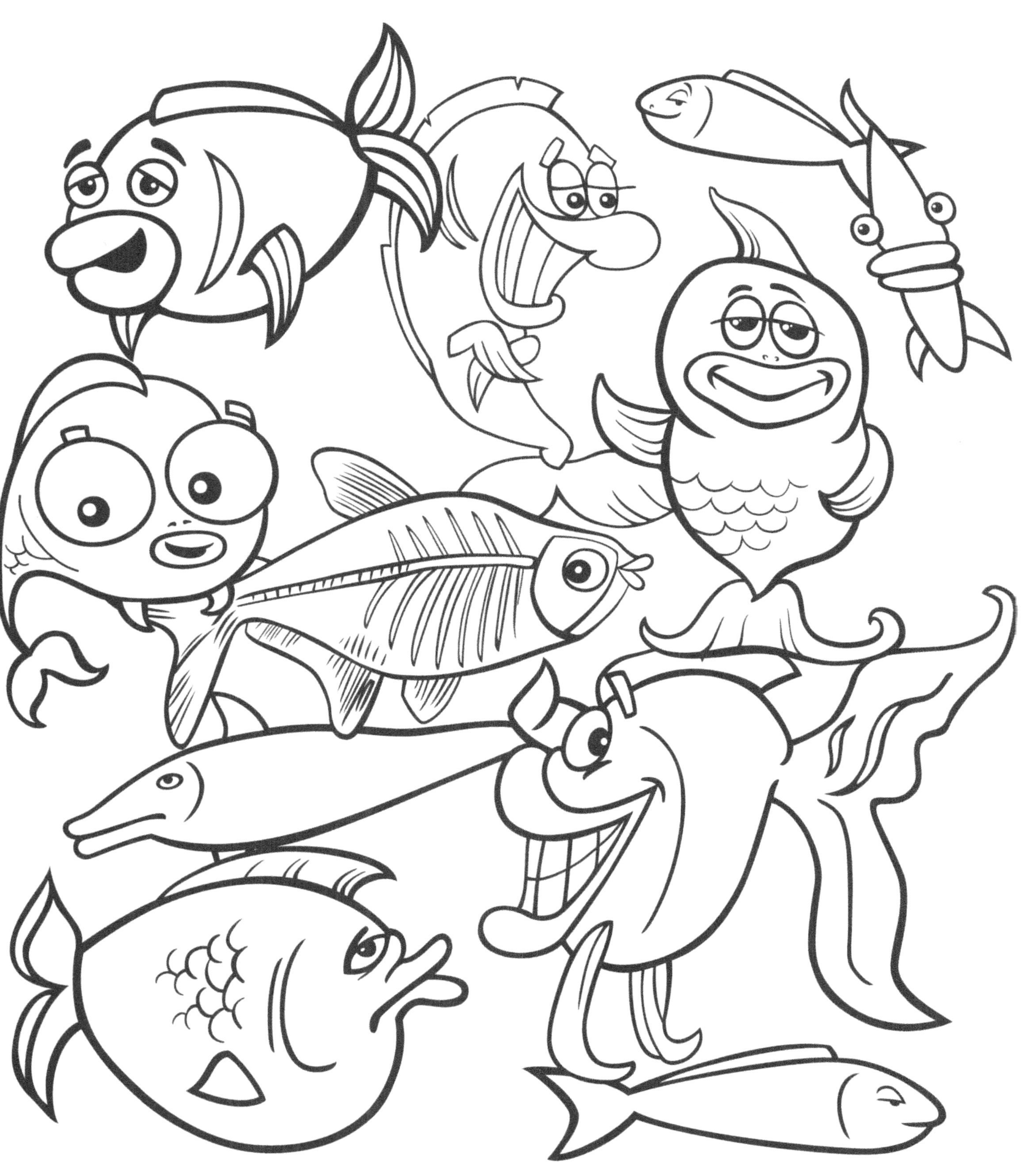

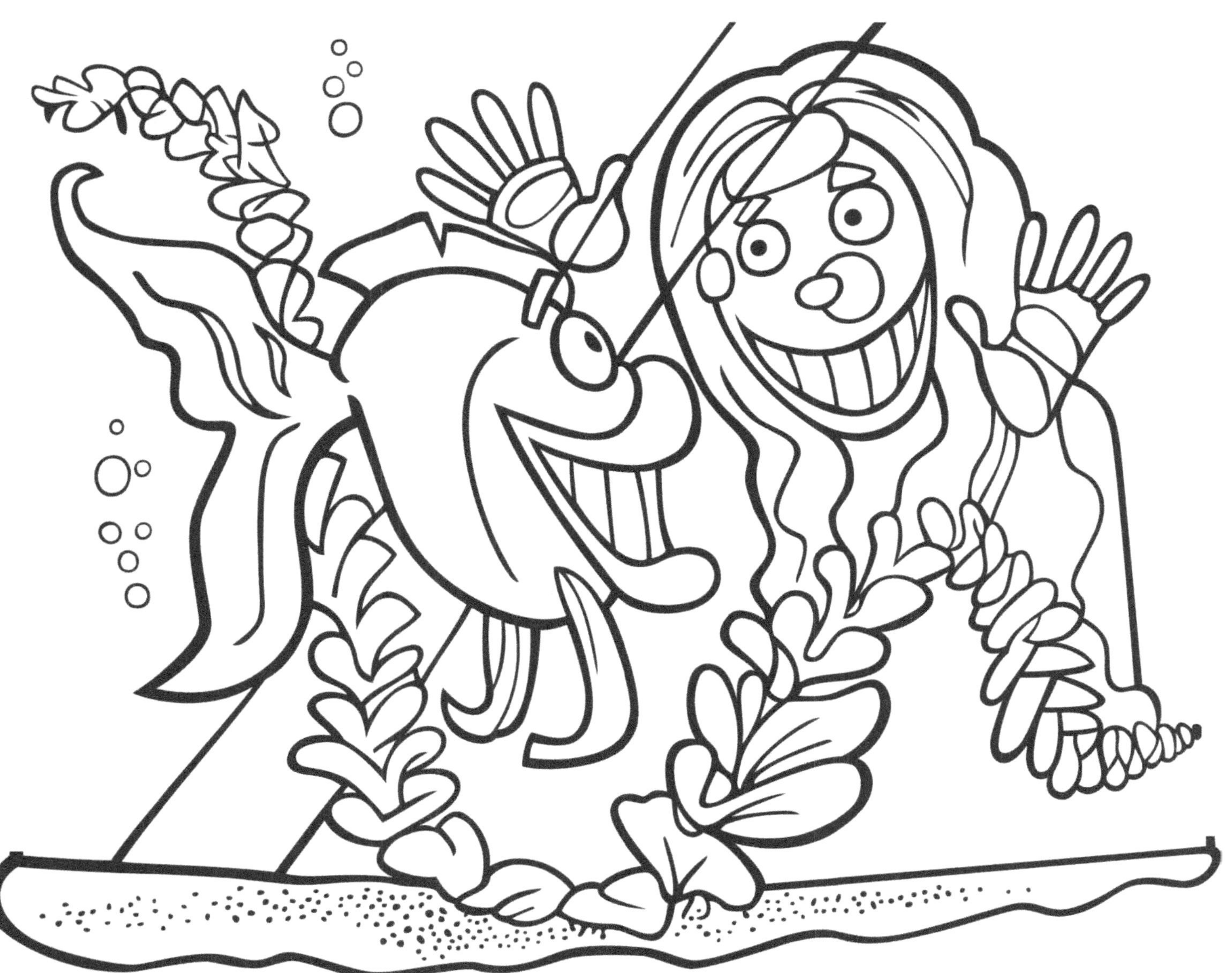

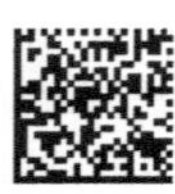

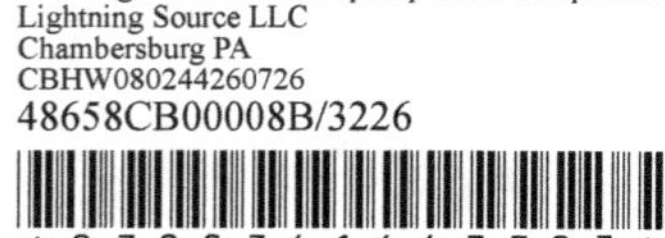
* 9 7 9 8 7 4 1 4 4 7 7 0 3 *